Mighty Machines
DUMP TRUCKS
and other
BIG MACHINES

Ian Graham

QED Publishing

First published in the UK in 2008 by
QED Publishing
A Quarto Group company
226 City Road
London EC1V 2TT

www.qed-publishing.co.uk

A Catalogue record for this book is available from the British Library.

ISBN 978 1 84538 929 1

Written by Ian Graham
Designed by Phil and Traci Morash (Fineline Studios)
Editor Paul Manning
Picture Researcher Claudia Tate
Publisher Steve Evans
Creative Director Zeta Davies
Editorial Manager Wendy Horobin

Printed and bound in China

Picture credits
Key: t = top, b = bottom, FC = front cover

Alamy/Justin Kase 5t, /South West Images Scotland 17t; **Corbis**/Construction Photography 21;
JCB/ 8, 11t; **Hochtief Aktiengesellchaft**/ 20b; **Komatsu**/ 14, 15; **Shutterstock**/Alexander Briel
Perez FC, /Bjorn Heller 1, /nialat 4, /Zygalski Krzysztof 6, /ownway 6b, /Brad Whitsitt 7t, /Ljupco
Smokovski 10, /Mark Atkins 12, /Florin C 13t, /Kamil Sobócki 16, /Mark Atkins 18, /Stanislav Komogorov
19a; **Volvo**/ 9t

Words in **bold** can be found
in the Glossary on page 23.

Contents

What is a dump truck?

Dump **trucks**, diggers, loaders and bulldozers are all types of **construction** vehicles. These big machines help to build roads, bridges, tunnels and tall buildings.

Some construction vehicles carry materials for building. Others have tools for digging, lifting and pushing.

These two diggers are being carried to work on the back of a transporter.

The huge back section of this dump truck can carry up to 136 tonnes of earth and rubble.

Diggers

Digging machines, or excavators, work by pushing a metal **bucket** into the ground so that it fills up with earth.

digging bucket

The biggest excavator in the world can dig an 18-metre-deep hole as big as a football pitch in just a day!

Big metal teeth on the front of the digging bucket help to break up the ground.

This vehicle is a **backhoe**. It has a bucket at the back for digging and legs to keep it steady.

driver's cab

Some excavators have **tracks** instead of wheels. Tracks spread the weight and stop the excavator from sinking into soft ground.

tracks

Trucks

Before building work can begin on a **construction site**, huge piles of earth and rubble may need to be shifted. Dump trucks and tipper trucks do this work.

Big trucks also deliver sand, gravel,
bricks and other building materials
to the construction site.

A tipper truck tips up
at the back to empty
its load onto
the ground.

Loaders

It would take a long time to fill a dump truck by hand! A machine called a loader can do the job much more quickly.

Smaller loaders are useful for working in awkward spaces.

A loader scoops up earth in a big, wide bucket. Then the bucket is lifted up over a truck and the earth is tipped into it.

As well as filling trucks, a loader's powerful arms can push earth and rubble along the ground like a bulldozer.

Concrete mixers

Construction work needs a lot of **concrete**. Concrete is made by mixing sand, stones and cement with water. Once the sloppy mixture has been poured, it sets as hard as a rock.

The drum of a mixer truck holds 18 tonnes of concrete — the weight of 12 mid-sized family cars!

drum

Concrete is brought to construction sites by mixer trucks. The concrete is carried in a big drum, which keeps turning to stop the cement from setting hard.

chute

On this mixer truck, the drum is emptied by pouring the concrete down a chute at the back.

Bulldozers

Bulldozers are big, powerful machines that are used to move earth and rubble. A blade at the front of a bulldozer scrapes up the earth and pushes it along in front.

blade

Bulldozers are used to clear the land to make it ready for building. They can flatten a big area very quickly.

Tracks help a bulldozer grip the ground and push hard.

tracks

15

Cranes on wheels

If a tall building is being constructed, materials and other heavy loads may have to be lifted high above the ground.

The **boom** is lowered when the crane is moving.

boom

On big construction sites tall cranes are kept busy all the time. On smaller sites, special **mobile** cranes are brought in when they are needed.

Strong legs called **outriggers** keep the crane from tipping over.

outrigger

Roadbuilders

Before a road can be built, the ground has to be made very flat. Bulldozers and machines called scrapers and graders are used to flatten the area.

A grader scrapes a blade along the ground to smooth out the bumps.

Then vehicles called pavement-layers, or pavers, can get to work.

To make the surface of a road, a pavement-layer uses a mixture of stones and hot, sticky **tar**.

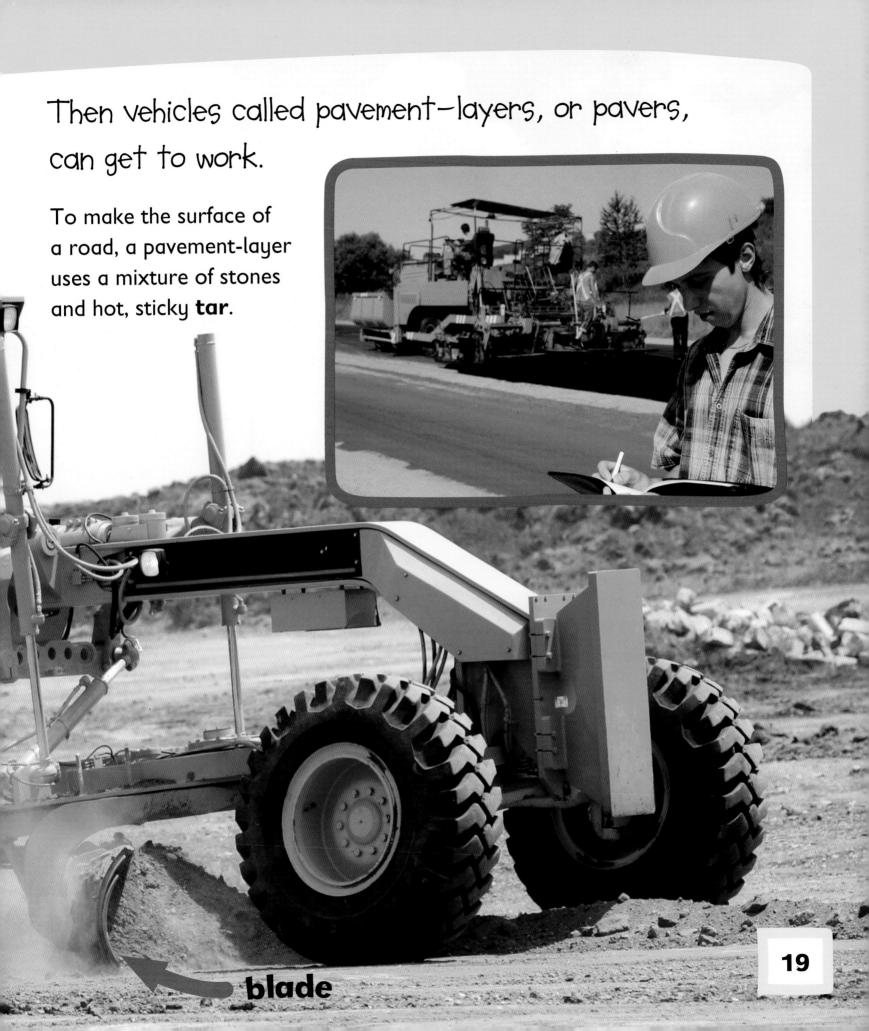

blade

Tunnellers

If a road or railway has to cross a river or a hill, the quickest way is often to dig a tunnel under it.

Long, underground tunnels are made by tunnel-boring machines. These rock-eating monsters cut their way through solid rock like long, metal worms.

A tunnel-boring machine can carve out 20 metres of finished tunnel a day.

The huge cutting head of this tunnel borer spins round to cut through rock and earth.

cutting head

Activities

- Here are two construction vehicles from the book. Can you remember which jobs they do?

- If you had to build a house, which construction vehicles would you need, and why?

- Make a drawing of your favourite construction vehicle. What sort of vehicle is it? What colour is it? Where is it? What is it doing? Who is driving it?

- Which of these pictures shows an excavator?

Glossary

Backhoe
A digging machine that works by pulling a bucket through the ground

Boom
The main arm of a crane, which is also called the jib

Bucket
The part of a digging machine that scoops earth out of the ground

Concrete
A mixture of sand, stones, cement and water that sets hard, used to make buildings

Construction
Another word for building

Construction site
A place where building work is done

Mobile
Able to move from place to place

Outrigger
A part that sticks out from the side of a construction machine to make it steadier or stop it from tipping over

Tar
A thick, black, oily, sticky liquid used to make the surface of a road

Tracks
Metal belts used by bulldozers and some other construction vehicles instead of wheels to spread the weight and stop them from sinking into soft ground

Truck
A big road or construction vehicle used for moving heavy loads

Index